Recipe for Murder

A thriller

J.D.Robins

GW00771392

Samuel French — London
New York - Toronto - Hollywood

ESSEX
COUNTY COUNCIL
LIBRARY

© 2003 by J.D.Robins

Rights of Performance by Amateurs are controlled by Samuel French Ltd, 52 Fitzroy Street, London W1T 5JR, and they, or their authorized agents, issue licences to amateurs on payment of a fee. **It is an infringement of the Copyright to give any performance or public reading of the play before the fee has been paid and the licence issued.**

The Royalty Fee indicated below is subject to contract and subject to variation at the sole discretion of Samuel French Ltd.

Basic fee for each and every
    performance by amateurs   Code K
    in the British Isles

The publication of this play does not imply that it is necessarily available for performance by amateurs or professionals, either in the British Isles or Overseas. Amateurs and professionals considering a production are strongly advised in their own interests to apply to the appropriate agents for written consent before starting rehearsals or booking a theatre or hall.

ISBN 0 573 01985 1

Please see page iv for further copyright information.

RECIPE FOR MURDER

First presented at the Woolacombe Repertory Theatre,
Devon, in 2001, with the following cast:

David Lawson	Richard Haydon
Beatrice Hayward	Carole Hughes
Kit Kelly	Julian Rouse
Claire Lawson	Wendy Morrall

Directed by Jillian Rowe
Designed by Terri Wooff
Lighting designed by Norman Courtnay

COPYRIGHT INFORMATION

(See also page ii)

This play is fully protected under the Copyright Laws of the British Common-wealth of Nations, the United States of America and all countries of the Berne and Universal Copyright Conventions.

All rights including Stage, Motion Picture, Radio, Television, Public Reading, and Translation into Foreign Languages, are strictly reserved.

No part of this publication may lawfully be reproduced in ANY form or by any means — photocopying, typescript, recording (including video-recording), manuscript, electronic, mechanical, or otherwise—or be transmitted or stored in a retrieval system, without prior permission.

Licences for amateur performances are issued subject to the understanding that it shall be made clear in all advertising matter that the audience will witness an amateur performance; that the names of the authors of the plays shall be included on all programmes; and that the integrity of the authors' work will be preserved.

The Royalty Fee is subject to contract and subject to variation at the sole discretion of Samuel French Ltd.

In Theatres or Halls seating Four Hundred or more the fee will be subject to negotiation.

In Territories Overseas the fee quoted above may not apply. A fee will be quoted on application to our local authorized agent, or if there is no such agent, on application to Samuel French Ltd, London.

VIDEO-RECORDING OF AMATEUR PRODUCTIONS

Please note that the copyright laws governing video-recording are extremely complex and that it should not be assumed that any play may be video-recorded for whatever purpose without first obtaining the permission of the appropriate agents. The fact that a play is published by Samuel French Ltd does not indicate that video rights are available or that Samuel French Ltd controls such rights.

CHARACTERS

David Lawson: research scientist; early 40s
Beatrice Hayward: his sister; mid-to-late 40s
Kit (Christopher) **Kelly**: journalist; early 40s
Claire Lawson: David's wife, a writer; mid-30s

The action of the play takes place in the sitting-room of the
Lawsons' country cottage

Time — the present

SYNOPSIS OF SCENES

ACT I
    Scene 1 A summer afternoon
    Scene 2 The following evening

ACT II
    Scene 1 The following morning
    Scene 2 Early afternoon the following day
    Scene 3 Half an hour later, the same afternoon

ACT 1

SCENE 1

The sitting-room of the Lawsons' cottage

A door L *leads to the rest of the cottage and french windows* R *lead into the garden. The room is comfortably furnished with a sofa, armchairs and occasional tables. There is a desk with a computer (plus printer) and a pot of pens and paintbrushes on it and a waste-paper bin beside it. Behind the sofa there is another table. Pot plants and ornaments — including a bowl — are dotted about*

When the CURTAIN *rises, the french windows are open and there is a folded newspaper on the arm of the sofa*

David enters from the garden. He is a quiet, studious man in his early forties. He carries a green foliage plant in a pot and a corked bottle containing some white liquid. He sits at the computer and puts the plant and the bottle on the desk beside him. He makes an entry on the computer and then lifts the plant to eye level and examines the foliage. He replaces the plant on the desk and lifts the bottle. He gives it a good shake and then removes the cork. He takes a paintbrush from the pot on the desk, dips it into the bottle and starts to paint the leaves of the plant

Beatie enters through the door L *carrying a tray of tea things, scones etc. She is a rather homely-looking woman a few years older than David. She places the tray on the table behind the sofa*

Beatie Tea, David. I'm sorry it's a bit late, but I got waylaid.
David (*concentrating on his plant*) Ah, tea.
Beatie The kettle was boiling and then the fish man called.
David (*preoccupied*) Good, good.
Beatie I had quite a go at him, I can tell you.
David Right.
Beatie He said he'd come to deliver some plaice. I never buy plaice myself. Too expensive, and not enough on it, I always think. I could see at a glance that it wasn't fresh, so I told him: "Don't you think you can palm me off with stale fish," I said. You could see he wasn't very pleased; you could tell.

Anyway, he went back to the van and got some very passable-looking haddock. Quite fresh, and much cheaper, what's more. I'll poach it in milk for your supper.

David (*his attention caught at last*) Poach it! In milk?

Beatie (*looking at her watch*) Oh dear! Forget my head next. It's time for your medicine. I'll just go and ——

David Beatie, stop bobbing up and down. Come and sit down, have some tea, have a scone.

Beatie Oh, no, dear. Don't tempt me, not on my diet sheet ... No, I'll just go ——

David Oh, come on, the medicine can wait.

Beatie That's just where you're wrong. The important thing with stomach ulcers is regularity.

David I do not have stomach ulcers!

Beatie That's what you say.

David A touch of indigestion now and again is not ulcers.

Beatie Indigestion, ulcers, whatever, it's the same thing, and you can't deny how much better you've been since I got here. Regular meals, that's what's done it. You keep such ramshackle hours. Never a meal at the same time two days running.

David I keep irregular hours, even when I'm working at home. We're used to it. It suits us. We hate set routines.

Beatie My poor Jim and I, we always sat down on the dot. Good plain food, that's what he liked. But you two, well! All that rich food, so fattening, and all those sauces, I can't tell what's under them half the time. And as for those spices, well, even the smell of all that garlic is enough ——

David I like tasty food.

Beatie I daresay you do, but it's never liked you. I remember when we were children. Whenever we went to a party you were sick.

David That was excitement, not garlic!

Beatie Too many cream buns, more like. Anyway, I shall tell Claire you've hardly had a twinge since she's been away. We'll have a nice little talk when she gets home this evening.

David Oh dear!

Beatie You needn't worry, I shan't upset her. I flatter myself I can speak plainly without giving offence.

David (*with foreboding*) I hope so.

Beatie You'll see, she'll be grateful for my advice. After all, her first husband didn't make old bones, did he?

David He didn't have stomach ulcers either.

Beatie No, well, the less said about that, the better. Anyway, it's a good job I'm here for a nice long visit this time.

Beatie bustles out

David stirs the contents of his bottle with the brush and goes back to painting the plant. He finds it awkward to get the brush into the narrow neck of the bottle and looks around for a more suitable container. He sees the teacups on the tray and gives a grunt of satisfaction. He takes a cup, pours some of the liquid from the bottle into it and continues painting. The painting is easier now

Beatie enters with a glass of medicine, also white in colour

Beatie Here now. Drink this down.

David Thank you, Beatie, I will in a minute.

Beatie No, David, now! Let me see you get it down.

David Oh, all right, if I must. (*He takes the glass, drinks the medicine down in one gulp and pulls a face*) Yuck!

Beatie Really, David, you do make a fuss, it's only bismuth. Here, I'll pour you some tea to take the taste away. (*She pours David a cup of tea*) I was just thinking: do you remember, Mother always said that ulcers were caused by worry.

Beatie takes David's tea to him

David That's nonsense, and anyway, even if I did have an ulcer, I don't have anything to worry about.

Beatie No? (*She heads back to the tea tray, glancing meaningfully at the newspaper on the arm of the sofa as she passes*) You've seen today's paper, then?

David Yes.

Beatie There's another of those articles about the Research Centre.

David Yes.

Beatie That's the third, isn't it?

David doesn't answer

Mrs Musgrove, down at the post office, says that until they find out who's writing them, everyone will be under suspicion. Even senior people, like you.

David Ah well, if Mrs Musgrove says so — who are we to disagree?

Beatie Oh, you can tease all you like, but I should say you had plenty to worry about.

David Beatie, when you work in that sort of establishment, you accept the fact that everyone's always under suspicion, all the time. You get used to it.

Beatie (*unconvinced*) Right ——

David Right. And we don't talk about it.

The doorbell rings

Beatie Now who could that be, I wonder?
David Only one way of finding out, go and let them in.

Beatie looks at David suspiciously, then realizes he's teasing her

Beatie Right, I'll go.

Beatie exits

David sips his tea absentmindedly. He picks up the brush and is just about to dip it into his tea when he realizes it's the wrong cup

Beatie enters, followed by Kit. He is about the same age as David and attractive in a florid sort of way

Beatie David, you've got a visitor. This is — I'm sorry, I'm hopeless — I didn't catch your name.
Kit Kit Kelly.
Beatie Right — this is my brother, David. (*Flustered in attractive male company*) David, Mr – er – Kelly? Did you say … ?
Kit Call me Kit, everybody does.
Beatie (*pleased*) Oh, Kit, then. David, Kit has just moved into Twopots Cottage.
David Have you? I heard that somebody had. Well, that makes us neighbours, then.
Kit Yes. I moved in last week, so I thought it was about time I introduced myself.
David Glad you did.
Beatie I'm sure that Claire would have dropped in to welcome you, wouldn't she, David?
David Yes, yes, I'm sure she would, she's been away, you see ——

The telephone rings, off

Oh, excuse me a minute.
Beatie I'll go, shall I?
David Why? Were you expecting a call, Beatie?
Beatie No, I just thought ——
David Well, if you're not, it might save time if I went.

David raises his eyebrows at Kit and exits

Beatie Oh, he's such a tease! Do sit down — er — Kit. Twopots Cottage, that's the one that's been empty for so long.

Kit Yes, in estate agent speak, it's "in need of certain renovation"! I haven't bought it though, just renting; see how I get on living in the country. Not my usual scene; I'm not sure I can take all this space and fresh air.

Beatie (*fishing*) And your wife?

Kit Ex-wife; I'm divorced.

Beatie (*brightening up at this information*) I see — so you're —— ?

Kit When she heard I was going to live in the country, that gave her a good laugh. Swore I wouldn't be able to put one foot in front of another without a pavement under my feet. This — from a woman who gets withdrawal symptoms if she's more than ten minutes from Harrods.

Beatie (*amused*) So, if you feel like that about the country, why take Twopots Cottage?

Kit It's a long way from Harrods!

Beatie Claire shops at Harrods ——

Kit Claire?

Beatie My sister-in-law. I went with her once, to Harrods, just for a look round; I didn't buy anything, of course.

Kit You went to Harrods and didn't buy anything? I've been looking for you all my life — will you marry me?

Beatie (*blushing; flirtatiously*) Why, Mr Kelly, I hardly know you.

Kit We can soon put that right.

Beatie is unused to coping with this sort of banter; she giggles

Beatie (*changing the subject*) What about the garden, at Twopots? It's very overgrown. Are you a keen gardener?

Kit Good God, no! I don't know a flower from a weed. I might get a flame-thrower.

Beatie A flame-thrower! Oh, I see, you're teasing again. You're as bad as David. Are you going to work up at the Centre?

Kit The Centre?

Beatie The Government Research Centre.

Kit Good gracious, no! I'm no scientist, I don't know one end of a Bunsen burner from another.

David enters

David That was Claire, she's staying another night. Coming home tomorrow.

Beatie Oh dear, does that mean that Mrs Thornton is worse?

David No, she's OK, I think.

Beatie (*looking at her watch*) I should have thought she might have rung before ...

David Beatie, don't you think … (*He indicates the tea tray*)
Beatie Oh, good heavens, of course, how rude of me. (*To Kit*) We were just having tea; will you have a cup? (*She moves to the tea tray*)
David Or something stronger if you prefer it.
Kit Oh yes, I'd much prefer it — but tea is fine. I'm supposed to be laying off the hard stuff.
Beatie Quite right too, and so should you, David, with that ulcer. (*She hunts for the other tea cup*) Funny, I could have sworn I brought two cups.
David (*indicating the cup on the desk*) Oh, sorry, it's over here.
Beatie What's it doing over there?

David hands Beatie the cup

Now then, Kit, how do you like your tea?
Kit Oh, just as it comes; two sugars, please.
Beatie Sugar?
Kit Yes, I know, just one of my bad habits, but I can't bear those sweetener things.
Beatie (*squinting into the cup*) David, did you put milk in this cup? I haven't got my glasses on.
David Milk?
Beatie Yes, did you put milk in the cup?
David No. (*He looks puzzled and then remembers*) No, not milk, sorry, I was using it for my defoliant.
Beatie What!
David I needed something to put it in.
Beatie You've been using a tea cup for one of your concoctions?
David It's a defoliant.
Beatie What is a defoliant?
David It kills the leaves on the plant.
Beatie Kills? You mean it's a poison?
David Only to the foliage. Quite harmless otherwise … Well, it might give you a bit of a pain.
Beatie David, how could you? I nearly gave it to Kit.
David Good job you noticed.
Beatie David, you really are … Supposing I hadn't noticed? It doesn't bear thinking about.
David Well, you did, didn't you? So no harm done.
Beatie That isn't the point.
David Why don't you get another cup, and one for yourself? Oh, and you can find the sugar and look for your glasses at the same time.

Beatie exits indignantly with the dirty cup

Sorry, she goes on a bit.

Kit Defoliants: are they your line of work?

David No, not really, just a little experiment of my own; could turn out to be quite useful in the garden. Not quite right though, needs some more work.

Kit But that *is* what they're doing at the Research Centre, isn't it? I hear you work there?

David Oh? Who told you that?

Kit I don't know, I heard it mentioned somewhere, in the pub I think. Is it supposed to be a secret?

David No, it isn't a secret, lots of people round here work there, and I daresay you'd meet most of them in the *Rose and Crown*. Apart from Mrs Musgrove at the post office, Harry at the *Rose and Crown* is the local authority on most things.

Kit I gather the Centre is one of those hush-hush establishments.

David doesn't answer

But just at the moment, not as hush-hush as they would like?

David We have these flaps every so often. (*He chuckles*) Security gets tighter than ever for a while, and even the colour of the cleaner's knickers is classified!

Kit Local gossip says that whoever is writing these articles must have an inside contact.

David Local gossip?

Kit Perhaps I should say, gossip at the local — you know, bar-room stuff.

David Ah.

Kit According to Harry, there's no doubt that the background is authentic, but as for the content — there's nothing there that isn't already in the public domain.

David Harry seems well informed.

Kit Then why all the fuss?

David Government projects are always touchy. No publicity is good publicity. They're all the same: once they get into power, it's "to hell with open government!" They get away with it by maintaining that national security is more important than the public's right to know.

Kit But you said there was nothing sensitive.

David I didn't say that; according to you, Harry did.

Kit But you don't deny that these articles don't contain any classified information?

David Not if Harry says they don't.

Kit So all it amounts to, then, is some clever research into already-published material. Old copy re-hashed?

David As far as I know, none of it is new. But you must understand, they'd rather not have attention drawn to the Centre. The more the government denies that anything sinister is going on up there, the more the public doesn't believe them — it's the old dilemma: how do you answer the question "when did you stop beating your wife?"

Kit But the local colour is genuine? It is an inside job?

David Not necessarily. The "local colour", as you call it, could be supplied by anyone with a connection to the Centre. That adds up to quite a few people, if you count the families of anyone who works there, in any capacity.

Kit Why do you suppose they are doing it?

David Money, I should imagine.

Kit Or a diversion?

David Diversion?

Kit Suppose there really was a leak; what better way of covering your tracks than creating a stink in another direction?

David Do you have some personal interest in all this? If your information comes entirely from the gossip at the *Rose and Crown*, why do I get the feeling I'm being grilled?

Beatie enters with clean cups and a sugar bowl. She carries on as if she'd never left the room

Beatie I tell you, Kit, the more I see of this household, the more I think they're both mad. You and Claire. She should insist that you make your messes out in the greenhouse. I don't know what she can be thinking of.

During the following, Beatie pours Kit's tea, puts two spoonfuls of sugar into the cup and takes it to him. She offers him a seat and he sits

David Claire is used to my "messes" as you call them. If she finds anything lying around she gives it an extra-special scrub.

Beatie She may do, but my eyesight isn't as sharp. Deadly poisons in the sitting-room! Mark my words, one of these days there's going to be a nasty accident in this house. When it happens, don't say you haven't been warned.

David No, dear, we won't.

Beatie Don't you agree, Kit, it's an accident just waiting to happen?

Kit (*not wishing to be drawn into a family argument and seeking to change the subject*) Have you ever heard of the theory which says there's no such thing as an accident?

David Yes, but I forget how it goes.

Kit If I remember rightly, it goes something like this: if an accident was caused by carelessness or incompetence, then it could have been foreseen and prevented; if it wasn't prevented, then perhaps someone actually wanted it to happen.

Beatie But nobody could want …

Kit It doesn't have to be consciously — or not necessarily; it could be unconsciously.

David You mean like being accident-prone?

Kit Exactly.

Beatie Accident-prone? I've never understood what that means.

David It means not looking where you're going, not noticing obvious hazards, moving without due care and attention.

Beatie But not all accidents are caused by someone *doing* something or *not* doing something.

Kit True, but in that case, it isn't just an accident, it's called an "Act of God"; even insurance companies make that distinction.

David I see what you mean.

Beatie Well, I can't say I do.

Kit Well, it's only a theory, a bit of fun.

Beatie Rubbish I'd call it. According to your theory, if I go out and get run over by a bus, it'll be my own fault because I wanted it to happen.

Kit You, or somebody else.

Beatie That's nonsense, call things by their proper names. If I fall under a bus because *I* want to, that's suicide; if I fall under a bus because somebody *else* wants me to, then that's murder.

David She's got a point there, wouldn't you say?

Kit Brilliant! A masterpiece of logic. Well done, Beatie. I tell you, there's many a case I've sat through and wished the judge could sum up as clearly as that.

Beatie Court case? Are you a lawyer, then? A barrister?

Kit Good God, no! (*He stands*) Well, I'd better be making a move. Wouldn't do to outstay my welcome on the first visit. Thanks for the tea.

David Oh, anytime.

Beatie It was lovely to meet you, wasn't it, David? What a pity you missed Claire. I know, why don't you come over tomorrow evening and meet her? If you're free, of course.

Kit Thanks, but some other time perhaps. (*To David*) I'm sure your wife won't want visitors on her first night home.

Beatie No, really, Claire loves company, doesn't she, David? She'd love to meet you, do come.

David, placed in an awkward position, is obliged to endorse the invitation

David Yes, do come; as Beatie says, Claire likes company.

Kit Well, if you're sure, thank you.

David After having spent nearly a week with her mother-in-law, she'll need cheering up.

Kit Your mother?

David What? Oh, no, not my mother. She's Claire's first husband's mother. It gets a bit confusing.

Kit Ah, Tomorrow evening, then.

David About eight?

Kit Fine, see you then.

Kit heads for the exit. David moves to see him out

Beatie Just a moment — if you're going to the end of the lane, you'll pass the post box. David, where's that envelope? The one Claire wanted posting? (*She starts to rummage around the desk*)

David Oh, we needn't bother him with that, Beatie, it's nothing important.

Beatie Of course it is. Claire said to be sure and post it today.

David Well, I'll pop down with it later.

Beatie Whatever for? Kit's going right past the box.

Kit It's no trouble, really.

Beatie (*finding a large brown envelope and giving it to Kit*) Here it is. It's to her agent. Claire is a writer, you know.

Kit Your wife is?

David Yes, she scribbles a bit, more of a hobby really.

Beatie Oh, how can you say that, David? She's had all sorts of things published.

David Women stuff mostly, you know the sort of thing — cookery tips, household hints.

Kit I look forward to meeting her.

Beatie This one is an article on cookery, she said.

David Twenty ways to cook with spices, eh, Beatie?

Beatie I shouldn't be at all surprised.

Beatie and Kit exit

David watches Kit go with a reflective expression. He picks up the newspaper and reads a few lines, and then drops it in the waste bin with an impatient gesture. He returns to the desk and examines the plant. Deprived of the teacup, he looks around for something else to pour his mixture into. He finds the medicine glass, rinses it out with some water from the hot water jug and pours the dregs into the nearest teacup. He fills the glass from the bottle and, happily, starts painting his plant once more

CURTAIN

SCENE 2

The following day. Evening

There is a tray of drinks and glasses on the table behind the sofa

David enters carrying a glass of the white medicine. He sips it and makes a face. He looks around for somewhere to dispose of it, then pours the medicine into a potted plant. He goes to the drinks tray, pours himself a brandy and sips it appreciatively

Claire enters. She is an elegant woman in her mid-thirties

Claire Ah-ha! Caught you at it!
David (*jumping and spinning round*) Oh! It's you. Thank God! I thought it was Beatie. Where is she?
Claire Clearing up. I left her to it. She's taken against the dishwasher and insists on washing everything by hand, in triplicate. God knows why. I can't get it through to her that the dishwasher sterilizes everything. I'll just let her get on with it — it's easier than arguing.
David She told you about the teacup?
Claire Several times.
David She means well.
Claire So I have to keep reminding myself. I'll have a brandy with you.
David Share mine, then if she comes in we can pretend it's yours.

David pours more brandy into the glass and hands it to Claire. From now on they share it, passing the glass back and forth

David Has Beatie been treating you to one of her "frank chats"?
Claire I'll say! (*Imitating Beatie*) "You know me, Claire. I've never been one to mince my words. I always think plain speaking is better." Plain speaking! What she calls plain speaking, most people would call rudeness, interference and downright impertinence.
David Poor darling.
Claire Every time she goes away, I forget how awful she is. Like toothache. She talks entirely in clichés. She must study them, like some people read books of quotations.
David What did she have to say?
Claire Apparently, I'm slowly poisoning you with a mixture of neglect and foreign cookery.
David I was rather looking forward to a spot of foreign cookery. What was that God-awful mess she served up for dinner?

Claire Boiled fowl in white sauce. Good for your ulcer.

David Now don't you start too. I haven't got an ulcer.

Claire Well, whatever you've got, she says it's been better since she put you on a diet. Is that true?

David A never-ending diet of coddled eggs and poached fish would starve anyone to death, let alone a self-respecting ulcer.

Claire What did the doctor say?

David Well, actually ...

Claire You haven't seen him, have you?

David I didn't like to bother him, specially since it seems to be getting better.

Claire Who's this strange man Beatie's inflicting on us? One of her lame ducks?

David No, far from it. He's living at Twopots Cottage. Beatie seemed rather taken with him and insisted that he should meet you, so I couldn't avoid inviting him.

Claire Why on earth would he want to meet me? If Beatie's taken to him we're unlikely to have much in common. What's he like?

David I'm not sure. To tell you the truth, I didn't really know what to make of him.

Claire Oh?

David He seemed perfectly pleasant, friendly even, but I realized, after he'd left, that he'd told us next to nothing about himself.

Claire What does he do?

David That's just it, he didn't say. He seemed fascinated by all the gossip about the Centre. Maybe I'm being fanciful, but I did wonder if he might be Special Branch.

Claire You mean he's here to investigate us? Put us under surveillance?

David I imagine so. We shall all be under surveillance. If I'm right about him.

Claire Oh, I say! Better not tell Beatie, I wouldn't put it past her to ask him outright!

Beatie is heard approaching, off. David quickly passes the glass to Claire and moves away

Beatie enters. She notices the glass immediately

Beatie Oh. I was going to ask if you wanted any coffee, Claire, but I see you've already started drinking ... .

Claire (*sweetly*) No coffee, thank you, Beatie.

Beatie If you've had your medicine, David, I'll get you a glass of milk.

David looks alarmed

Claire David doesn't like milk, thank you, Beatie.

Beatie But it's so good for him, and since you've been away …
Claire (*smiling pleasantly*) But I'm back now, aren't I?

Beatie is about to protest, but seeing Claire smiling she decides to ignore the snub

Beatie Well, I expect you know best. (*Pause*) Tell me, how did you find poor old Mrs Thornton?
Claire Rather frail I'm afraid, but she's made a good recovery after her fall.
Beatie I've always thought it was so kind of you to be so good to your late mother-in-law.
Claire Mrs Thornton is still alive, Beatie. It's her son, my first husband, who is *late*.
Beatie Well, you know what I mean. It isn't as if you were any relation — not a blood relation, that is. Where are her own family?
Claire She hasn't any.
Beatie (*with meaning*) Ah, well, that's different, of course. Still it must be lonely for her, living alone and not being able to get out much. I expect she enjoyed having you there for an extra night.
Claire Oh, I didn't stay last night with Mother Thornton.
Beatie (*feeling she's on to something*) You didn't?
Claire No. I was in London, with a friend.
Beatie A friend?
Claire (*ignoring Beatie's interest*) Mother Thornton wanted me to see her solicitor.
Beatie Her solicitor? I daresay Mrs Thornton is quite comfortably off?
Claire (*ignoring the implication*) We went to the theatre last night and I had time to get my hair done this morning.
David And very nice it looks, darling.

Beatie is about to pursue her enquiries when the doorbell rings

Beatie That will be Kit, I'll go.

Beatie exits

Claire Kit! You'd think she'd invented him.
David Darling, try to be patient.
Claire I am trying, and so far I think I've succeeded admirably. How long is she staying?
David She said something about one of her nice long visits.
Claire Oh, God!
David Well you can't blame me, you invited her.

Claire To look after you while I was away, not to take root.

Beatie enters with Kit as if she were producing a rabbit out of a hat

Beatie Here he is, right on the dot. I do like punctuality.
Kit Not too punctual, I hope. My wife — my ex-wife — makes a point of being five minutes late.
David Nice to see you. Claire, darling, this is our new neighbour, Kit Kelly. Kit, my wife Claire.

It is obvious that Kit recognizes Claire. Claire looks uncomfortable and ill at ease, as if he looks familiar, but she can't place him

Kit How do you do? (*He deliberately goads her*) Have we met somewhere?
Claire No, I don't think so. (*She brazens it out*) I'm sure I should have remembered, I'm good at faces.
Kit I just had this feeling that you looked familiar.

During the following Kit keeps glancing at Claire, but she ignores him

Claire Perhaps I remind you of someone.
Beatie That's always happening to me. I remember we had a milkman once who was the spitting image of Uncle Edward. You recall him, David.
David No, I don't think I ever met your milkman, Beatie.
Beatie Not the milkman! I mean Uncle Edward.
David Oh yes, I remember Uncle Edward.
Claire But if David never saw your milkman, Beatie, there's little point to the story.
Beatie (*somewhat put out*) No, I suppose not. Kit, let me get you a drink.
Claire (*doing her best to be tactful*) You sit down, Beatie, you've been on the go all the evening. I'll do it. (*To Kit*) What can I get you?
Kit Scotch please, just a drop of water.
Claire Scotch and water. How about you, Beatie?
Beatie Oh, no, nothing for me, thank you, I really shouldn't.
David Oh, come on, Beatie, forget the diet for one night, have something, treat yourself.
Beatie Well, perhaps a small brandy; my poor Jim always said it was good for the digestion.

Claire moves to the drinks table, giving a relaxed "good hostess" performance. Kit watches her with interest. Claire pours Kit his Scotch and water and hands it to him. She starts to pour Beatie's drink

Oh dear! Oh no, just a small one, oh my, just look at all those calories.

Claire hands Beatie her drink

Oh well, might as well be hung for a sheep as a lamb. Cheers!

Claire What about you, David?

Beatie No, he mustn't.

Claire David?

David I'll have a brandy with Beatie; after all, she's just said it was good for the digestion.

Claire pours a brandy for David and hands it to him, then refills her own glass

Claire Cheers then! So, Mr Kelly ——

Kit Oh, Kit, please.

Claire Kit then, well how do you like ... Kit? ... Christopher? (*The penny drops*) You're Christopher Kelly, aren't you?

Kit That's right.

Claire Do you hear that, David? We have a celebrity living next door.

David Of course, good Lord! *That* Christopher Kelly?

Kit The one and only.

Beatie What are you talking about?

Claire Kit's a journalist, Beatie, a rather well-known one.

Beatie Really? Well, how exciting. You never said.

David A journalist! And now we've blown your cover.

Kit Cover?

David Yes. I never thought of a journalist. I had you down for an undercover policeman!

Kit What, me? A policeman!

David I suppose you didn't say who you were because you're here to write about the Centre.

Kit Believe it or not, but it's gospel truth, I didn't even know that the Research Centre was just up the road until after I'd moved in. I didn't mention it because I'm not working at the moment.

Claire Oh? So what's the attraction of Twopots Cottage?

Kit I thought this was the sort of place where nothing ever happened, and as I've been ordered to take a complete rest, it seemed ideal.

Beatie Ordered?

Kit My doctor. I've had a spot of heart trouble. Been one of those years, work, divorce ... Anyway, he says I've got to change my ways, what he calls my "unhealthy lifestyle". Lots of sleep, exercise, no smoking and no booze ...

David looks quizzically at Kit's glass of Scotch

Yes, I know, but you can't do it all at once, and I haven't smoked for a week.

David So, you're not writing about the Centre, then?

Kit I can't say I haven't been tempted. Think of the headline: "Scientists and their families under cloud of suspicion. Who is the mole in our midst?"

David Oh, Lord!

Kit However, just this evening I've had an idea for a "human interest" piece. Might even be a series in it.

Beatie Human interest?

Kit "Where are they now?"

David How do you mean?

Kit Well, haven't you noticed, a person can be on all the front pages for a day or two, then suddenly something else grabs the headlines. Haven't you ever wondered what happens to those people? One minute they're household names, and the next it's as if they'd never existed. I thought it might be fun to trace one, find out what they are doing now. (*He looks at Claire, studying her reaction*)

Claire merely smiles

David Would anyone be interested?

Kit They might; you'd have to chose carefully. Pick someone who'd made a big impression during their five minutes of fame.

Beatie If I were you, I'd write about all those court cases you were talking about. Have you done any murders trials? Everyone likes to read about those.

David That's right, a slim volume: "Mass Murderers I Have Known" — make a nice little stocking-filler.

Kit Not more mass murders, they've been done to death!

David and Claire laugh politely. Beatie laughs uproariously

Beatie You are a scream — "done to death!" But people are interested in mass murderers, you know, because they're mad.

Kit Not according to the law.

Beatie Well, I don't care what the law says. I mean, they aren't normal, are they? I mean, it isn't normal to want to kill people, is it?

David Don't you find them psychologically interesting?

Kit Not really.

David Then what sort of murder do you find interesting?

Kit There is a particular type of domestic murder which I find fascinating. One committed in cold blood, by someone who's clever, calculating, and completely sane.

David Isn't that rare?

Kit Not as rare as you might think. But often, you don't hear about them.

David You mean they go undetected?

Kit Not exactly; there may be strong suspicion, but if the police can't find the evidence to make an arrest — then it may be impossible to prove that it was murder.

Beatie Why?

Kit Because it looks like an accident.

Beatie Oh, go on! Now we're back to your accident theory.

Kit That was just a bit of fun about spontaneous accidents. Murders disguised to look like accidents have to be very carefully planned.

Claire Well, if they're that clever, there shouldn't be any suspicions.

Kit There aren't in many cases, but my police contacts tell me that they develop a sort of intuition.

David Oh, come on, are you saying the police have second sight?

Kit No, of course not, there's nothing mystical about that sort of intuition. It comes from experience and trained observation.

David Trained observation?

Kit We all have it, in some form or another. Take you, for instance, you are a highly qualified and experienced research chemist. If someone showed us both a complicated formula, you'd understand it and I wouldn't. Nothing mystical about that.

David Right, so the police suspect that it wasn't an accident. What happens next?

Kit The usual; they look for a motive. Who benefits? Who had the opportunity? In a domestic setting there is always plenty of opportunity.

Claire What sort of opportunity?

Kit Well, take this household ...

Claire What, us?

Kit Certainly. You weren't here yesterday, Claire, but the others will remember. David used a tea cup to mix a chemical. Beatie noticed it, so there was no harm done. However, suppose she hadn't noticed it, suppose she'd drunk her tea from that cup?

David It wouldn't have hurt her, I told you.

Kit I know, but just for the sake of my argument, let's say it was poison.

David OK, OK, so it was poison — then what?

Kit An enquiry would have found you guilty of carelessness and negligence but without a motive it would have gone down as an accident.

David But that's exactly what it would have been, an accident.

Kit All right, but suppose — oh, I don't know — suppose they found out you were in debt and Beatie'd left you money? There you are: a motive.

David It could be ... but it might be ... just coincidence.

Kit Exactly, that's what I meant when I said that these cases are notoriously hard to prove. Chances are, whatever the suspicion, you'd get away with it, especially the first time and especially if you were a woman.

Beatie A woman?

Kit Statistically, the domestic murderer is more likely to be a woman.

Claire (*not at all happy with the turn of conversation, but seeming unconcerned*) Why is that?

Kit Because even in these liberated times, the home is still looked upon as a woman's natural setting. She has every reason to be there and endless opportunity.

Beatie But you said "the first time". Surely, if someone got away with it once, they wouldn't risk doing it again?

Kit I suspect that most wouldn't push their luck, but it has been known.

David I should have thought the police would be very suspicious, if they found the same person involved in a convenient accident for a second time.

Kit They would be, if they knew about the first time.

David They'd be bound to.

Kit Not necessarily. Think about it. Years may have gone by — people move on, change their names. All right, the killer has to take a calculated risk, but often it pays off.

Beatie But why? Why risk it?

Kit It must seem worth it, I suppose. Perhaps it becomes a habit, a convenient way of solving life's awkward problems.

Beatie Some must get caught, though. They can't all get away with it, not indefinitely.

Kit The ones who are caught are the ones we hear about. It's usually vanity and over-confidence that finally gives them away. As I said, they become creatures of habit and start to repeat themselves.

Beatie Repeat themselves?

During the following, David is silent and shows increasing signs of discomfort

Kit Not exactly, of course, but similarities, little details, circumstances … It only takes someone to spot those similarities and a pattern starts to emerge.

Beatie Someone spots a pattern … You mean a policeman? How? What pattern?

Kit That takes us back to his experiences and training. How can I explain it? You are an experienced cook, right? Now, if I were to show you a list of ingredients, and nothing else, you could soon make an educated guess at the rest of the recipe. Well, it's the same thing: an experienced investigator will recognize the recipe for murder.

Claire Have you ever come across a case like this, as a journalist, I mean?

Kit Oh yes, one in particular has bugged me for years.

Claire Oh? Why is that?

Kit Because, so far, the killer has never been brought to justice.

Claire How extraordinary. You've finished your drink, let me top you up. How about you, David?

David hunches over, clutching his middle, obviously in pain

David? Are you all right, what's the matter?

David It's nothing, darling. Nothing, it's passing.

Beatie Oh dear! Here we go again. I told you not to have that brandy, but no, you would have it. Nobody listens to me.

David I'm all right, Beatie, stop fussing.

Beatie But you're not all right, look at you. You've been as right as rain all the time Claire's been away and now you go and spoil it all on her first night home.

Claire Yes, well, never mind all that now, Beatie.

Beatie I'll get you some medicine.

Claire (*moving towards the door*) Don't bother, I'll go.

Beatie It's no bother, my dear.

Claire Sit down, Beatie, I'm half-way there.

Claire exits

Kit What is this medicine they've prescribed?

Beatie It wasn't prescribed. I just got some bismuth stuff from the chemist.

Kit You mean you haven't seen a doctor?

Beatie He's so naughty, he won't go.

Kit Look, it's no business of mine, old chap, but you should see a doctor. Tricky things, ulcers — besides, suppose it isn't an ulcer?

David It isn't an ulcer, just a bit of acid indigestion.

Kit Maybe, but take my advice: see a doctor, don't delay. They have miracle drugs for this sort of thing these days.

David I know, that's what Claire keeps telling me.

Kit Really? Well, I must be on my way — I'm supposed to be having early nights.

David But you were going to have another drink.

Kit We'll leave it for another time. I warn you, you'll soon be sick of me up here, attacking your bottle of Scotch. 'Night, Beatie, sweet dreams.

Beatie Well, if you must go ... I have enjoyed it. I shall go to bed and dream of murderers I expect.

Beatie escorts Kit to the door

Claire enters with the medicine

Claire Oh, not leaving us, are you, Mr Kelly? So early? I thought you were going to have another drink and entertain us with some more of your fascinating murder theories.

Kit Thanks, but I must go. Actually, our discussion has given me an idea. I
think I shall look up some old files before I turn in. Good-night, Claire, and
thanks for the drink.

Kit exits followed by Beatie

Claire looks rattled and deep in thought

Claire (*giving David the medicine*) Come along, David, drink this down. I
hate to admit it, but I think Beatie's right; you shouldn't drink brandy.
David (*sipping the medicine*) Interesting sort of chap, isn't he?
Claire Who, Kit Kelly? I suppose so, not really my type, too full of himself
I thought.
David Exaggerates a bit, perhaps. Obviously likes an audience — you could
see how Beatie was lapping it up. Hanging on his every word.

Claire takes the medicine glass from David

Claire You haven't finished it.
David I've had enough, I feel a bit sick.
Claire (*coaxingly*) Drink it down, darling. For my sake.

CURTAIN

ACT II

SCENE 1

The following day. Mid-morning

The room is empty and the french windows are open. The sound of a vacuum cleaner comes from beyond the door L

Kit appears in the window. He is carrying a straggly bunch of garden flowers

Kit Hallo? Anyone at home? (*He ventures into the room and moves to the door* L) Ahoy there, me hearties! Anyone there? (*He strolls back in the direction of the window. Passing the desk, he can't resist a quick rummage and presses a few keys on the computer*)

The sound of the vacuum cleaner stops. There comes the sound of Beatie approaching the inner door. Kit hears Beatie and moves back to the window

Beatie enters wearing her apron and with a duster in her hand

Kit coughs from the window

Kit Morning.
Beatie Oh, good gracious! I didn't see you there.
Kit Sorry, didn't mean to make you jump. I rang the bell but nobody answered, so I came round the side; thought you might be in the garden.
Beatie I didn't hear the bell, I was upstairs with the Hoover. David and Claire are out.
Kit I just strolled over to say thank you for last night ... Oh, and I picked these for you.

Kit gives the bunch of flowers to Beatie

Beatie Oh, aren't they lovely?
Kit Haven't a clue what they are, but there's masses of them in the garden.
Beatie Thank you. (*She sneezes violently*)
Kit David's out, you say? How is he? I didn't like the look of him last night.
Beatie He wasn't much better this morning. Claire's driven him down to the doctor's. (*She sneezes again*)

Kit Oh, Lord. Don't say it's the flowers.

Beatie So lovely, but so full of pollen. I'll just take them out. Don't go, sit down; I'll be right back.

Beatie exits through the door L

Kit moves back to the computer and presses a few keys

The sound of Beatie returning can be heard. Kit hears this and hurriedly sits on the sofa

Beatie enters

Of course he won't have it that it's an ulcer. But there, I'm not allowed to know anything. Father was just the same. You'd think David would remember, because it does run in families. Mother always said that ulcers were a matter of temperament. Caused by stress. I know that's not the modern view, but David does have such a responsible job …

Kit At the Research Centre?

Beatie Yes. Goodness knows what they do up there, he never speaks about it. Very hush-hush. Mind you, I don't suppose I'd understand if he told me. Bobbins they used to call them.

Kit Boffins.

Beatie What? Oh yes, boffins. Trust me to get it wrong, but then David got all the brains in the family. Just as well — he needed them, for all those scholarships and things. My parents couldn't have afforded to keep him at college and university for so many years. I've always been very proud of the way he managed. They were proud of him too, of course. It broke their hearts when he decided to stay in America after he'd finished his studies. Course, they're both dead now. I was surprised when he suddenly came back to England. I thought he'd stay in California.

Kit How long was he there?

Beatie Oh, years.

Kit What made him come back? Did Claire not like the American way of life?

Beatie Oh, Claire wasn't out there with him; they met after he returned.

Kit He hadn't been married before?

Beatie Oh, dear me, no. Confirmed bachelor, I thought he was. There was a girl once, I believe, while he was at university. I never met her, but it didn't work out. I don't know why — well, you don't like to ask, do you? But Mother always said that was why he decided to do his PhD in California. No, I really thought he would never marry.

Kit You don't live here all the time, then?

Beatie Oh, good heavens, no. I've got my own little place in Hove. Quite select, you know. I do get a bit lonely sometimes, on my own. David came home from America just after I lost my dear Jim, and I did think for a while that he and I might … But then he married Claire.

Kit How long are you staying here with them?

Beatie Claire asked me to come and look after David while she was away, but now she's back I shall stay on for a while. I know they enjoy having me here. I do the cooking and the cleaning. It makes a break for Claire. She doesn't like housework much, and it gives her more time to write.

Kit You sound as if you're fond of her.

Beatie Oh, yes, well I do admire her, she's so charming and clever. Men admire her too, I've noticed that. I must admit that when David first introduced her and said they were going to be married, I was a bit surprised. I remember thinking that she wasn't his type at all; I couldn't see what they had in common. I mean, David enjoys his work and loves a quiet life in the country, but, to be truthful, I think she gets a bit bored down here and likes to get away to her smart friends in London. They're all rolling in money, and of course, Claire has always been used to nice things. I don't mean that David's hard up, or anything, and of course Claire has her writing, but I can see that it worries him sometimes.

Kit So Claire has expensive tastes?

Beatie Well, I wouldn't put it like that exactly, but you see her first husband was rich and successful, and she always had the best that money can buy. Still, money doesn't buy happiness, does it?

Kit She was unhappy?

Beatie Claire's had such a sad life, you wouldn't believe how sad.

Kit Sad?

Beatie One thing after another, tragic. That's why I make allowances when she's a bit — well, you know — sharp. I always think an unhappy childhood affects people in later life, don't you?

Kit What happened?

Beatie As far as I can make out, her mother died when she was quite young.

Kit And her father?

Beatie I've never heard her speak of him. Perhaps he deserted them, or maybe her mother was — well, you know — on her own. That sort of thing doesn't matter now, of course. Anyway, her grandmother brought her up; she was devoted to Claire. You can imagine the loss it must have been to a young girl when she died. Such a shock.

Kit A shock?

Beatie Oh, yes, terrible. It was Claire who found her, you see. There were only the two of them living in the house.

Kit Claire found her?

Beatie Such a tragic accident. She'd been dead for hours, there was nothing anyone could do. The gas fire must have blown out while she was asleep. Careless thing to do, fall asleep with the fire on. You remember how dangerous they were, those old gas fires?

Kit Dreadful. What happened then?

Beatie Well, the poor child was on her own, she had nobody. I've no idea what her grandmother's circumstances were, but there must have been enough for her to finish her education. I think she married quite young.

Kit What was he like?

Beatie I never met him, of course. Judging by his photograph, he was a good-looking man, and as I said, very successful, a property dealer. But I had the impression that it wasn't always a happy match. Still, he was the last person on earth you would have expected to commit suicide.

Kit He committed suicide?

Beatie They said it was an accidental overdose. They always say that, don't they? Easier for the family. It used to be, "while the balance of mind was disturbed", but I never understood what that meant.

Kit What made him do it?

Beatie His business was in trouble. The fraud squad was called in and there was some sort of court case. I don't know the details, but it was in all the papers. We didn't know Claire then, of course, so we didn't pay much attention.

Kit Was he convicted?

Beatie He died in the middle of it. Couldn't face it I suppose. Preyed on his mind, poor man.

Kit And poor Claire.

Beatie Oh yes, by the time they'd cleared up all his affairs, I don't think there was much left. His creditors got most of it, I understand.

Kit As you say, an unusually sad life.

Beatie She never talks about it. I've pieced it together from things she's let drop and what David's told me. She still keeps in touch with Mrs Thornton, her first husband's mother. I think she may have expectations there. Poor old soul, I don't think she'll be with us much longer, the way she keeps falling about.

Kit Claire has been lucky with legacies, wouldn't you say?

Beatie I suppose she has. But it doesn't make up for other things, does it?

Claire enters through the door L. *She is not pleased to see Kit*

Beatie starts guiltily, realizing that she has been less than discreet

Claire Oh, Mr Kelly, what can we do for you?

Kit Just a neighbourly call to say "Hi", and thank you for last night.

Claire There was no need, I assure you.

Beatie Claire, Kit brought you some flowers from his garden.
Claire How extravagant.
Beatie And he enquired about David.
Claire How thoughtful.
Beatie Where is David?
Claire I dropped him off at work. He'll get a lift home this evening.
Beatie Won't he be home for lunch?
Claire He said he'd grab a sandwich in the canteen.
Beatie That's so bad for him. He needs regular meals.
Claire You tell him. I've given up.
Beatie What did the doctor say?
Claire Just what we thought, a suspected ulcer.
Beatie What is he going to do about it?
Claire He's got to have some tests.
Beatie When?
Claire As soon as they can arrange it; next week, probably.
Beatie Claire, I don't know how you can take it all so calmly. If it were my husband I'd be worried sick.
Claire Beatie, you do not hold a monopoly on worry.
Beatie (*offended*) No, no, of course not. Oh, good gracious, look at the time, I haven't finished upstairs yet. I must get on. (*She gets up*) Goodbye, Kit.
Kit Oh yes, bye, Beatie, I enjoyed our little chat.
Beatie Yes, well, you don't want to take too much notice of me, I sometimes run on a bit.

Beatie exits

There is a pause

Kit You must be relieved to have David's trouble diagnosed at last.
Claire What did you really come here for, Mr Kelly? To enquire after my husband, or to pump my sister-in-law?
Kit Pump! What a dreadful expression. Now why would I do that?
Claire Because that's how you earn your living, Mr Kelly.
Kit Could we drop the "Mr Kelly" bit, please? You've made your point.
Claire Point?
Kit That you aren't keen on having me for a neighbour. I wonder why?
Claire Because I get the impression that you're taking more than a neighbourly interest in my affairs. Almost a professional interest, I might say.
Kit I find you a very interesting woman, Claire.
Claire I realized last night that you recognized me, of course.
Kit I recognized you immediately. It obviously took you a bit longer to place me.

Claire I recognized the name, not the face. When one has been the object of press attention, you don't distinguish between one snarling hound and another.

Kit (*laughing*) Ouch! So, if you insist on calling me Mr Kelly, I shall call you Mrs — Thornton, perhaps?

Claire Whatever amuses you.

Kit After I left here last night, I did a bit of reading-up on the Thornton case, just to refresh my memory.

Claire You needn't have bothered. You could have asked me. In any case, it's common knowledge. My first husband, Nigel Thornton, died from an overdose of sleeping pills. The coroner had to decide whether it was suicide or an accident. He decided it was an accident.

Kit He never considered the other possibility.

Claire Oh? And what was that?

Kit Murder.

Claire Murder? Who could possibly have murdered him?

Kit The wife is usually the prime suspect.

Claire Me? — I mean, I? And how, exactly, was I supposed to have done that? "Come along, darling, wash your overdose down with your cocoa, and I'll tuck you in"?

Kit Something rather like that, I imagine. Nigel Thornton had been out drinking with a mate. The coroner concluded that he had come home, taken sleeping pills and gone to bed. Later, he is supposed to have woken and taken more pills by mistake. But you could have woken him, told him he'd forgotten his pills and given him more. In his drowsy state he would have done whatever you told him.

Claire You can't be serious. Do you really think he wouldn't have been suspicious, if I'd woken him from a deep sleep and offered him — a sleeping pill?

Kit He might not have realized that it was a sleeping pill — he was on other medication — and, as I say, he'd been drinking: when you're half-cut, one capsule looks much like another.

Claire This is fascinating, do go on.

Kit You became almost an obsession with me during your husband's trial. Did you know that?

Claire Am I supposed to be flattered?

Kit Fraud cases are unbelievably boring, so I used to while away the time watching you. You were — perfect. So calm and collected. A different outfit every day, always discreet, in the best of taste. I used to be there every morning to watch you arrive on your husband's arm, smiling serenely, confident of his innocence. The perfect wife. I used to watch the jury too. They couldn't take their eyes off you. I'm sure they didn't understand half of what was going on, but you could see what they were thinking: "How could this charming woman possibly be married to a crook?". Oh yes, they believed in you all right. At one stage, I thought you might almost bring off an acquittal.

Claire If I was hoping the jury would acquit him, why would I have killed him before the verdict? Your reasoning escapes me.

Kit Because the case against him was damning, and you knew he was guilty. You couldn't rely on the sympathy of that jury. You had to face the fact that he was going down for a long time, and where would that leave you? Out on your ear. So you decided to cut your losses and salvage the little you could before his creditors grabbed the lot.

Claire I'm speechless! How could you possibly have jumped to such a fantastic conclusion?

Kit Actually, I didn't jump to it, not then. It dawned on me slowly, much later. When the Thornton trial ended so abruptly with the death of the defendant, I felt it would round things off if I covered the inquest. There you were again, Claire, bewitching the court. Not the loyal, devoted wife this time, of course, but the tragic widow, so sad, so brave. Black suits you, and that little hat, with the wisp of veil … Absolute masterpiece. It was because you'd never put a foot wrong that it came to me for the first time: you were just too good to be true. Could anyone be that perfect? I began to ask myself. I decided to do a bit of digging of my own.

Claire And just where did you go to dig dirt?

Kit I started with your neighbours; I went to see the old lady who lived opposite.

Claire What on earth could she know? I'd never even spoken to her.

Kit So she said. As it happens she admired you from afar. Your comings and goings gave her something to look forward to.

Claire Nosy old cat!

Kit Very likely, but she did enjoy watching your exciting life — especially the other man.

Claire What other man?

Kit She didn't know who he was, but she'd seen him around for some weeks, coming to the house only when your husband was out. Ever so romantic she thought it was. She hadn't much time for your husband, thought he was a bit "flash", felt you deserved better. Now lover-boy, she liked the cut of his jib. Can you believe it? A respectable old dear like that? The things people tell you!

Claire It must be the cheque books you wave at them. She was obviously a lonely old soul who'd overdosed on Mills and Boon. She made him up, can't you see that? Did anyone else ever see him? Did you ever trace him?

Kit Not a trace. It's my guess that he ran out at the first sign of trouble —was that it, Claire?

Claire Why ask me? It's your fantasy, not mine. The tea-time gossip of a lonely old woman, and a man you can't prove ever existed: is this all you've got against me?

Kit No, but it was enough to convince me that further investigation was called for. I decided to look further back. And what did I find? Another inquest, but the same star witness. And the verdict? Your grandmother's death was an accident.

Claire What has my grandmother got to do with it?

Kit It made me wonder why sudden, tragic, accidental death should dog your footsteps.

Claire There's no connection.

Kit Oh, but there is — you are the connection. Now this will interest you: I spent the day in your old home village. Well, it's hardly a village any more, grown so much you wouldn't recognize the place. Most disappointing, I couldn't find anyone who'd lived there long enough to remember you. I'd almost given up when someone said that the vicar's wife was a local girl, and perhaps she could help. She remembered you, all right. It seems you were at school together.

Claire What was her name?

Kit Mrs Millicent Temple — you knew her as Millie Clegg.

Claire Millie Clegg? Good God! (*She starts to laugh*) Millie, a vicar's wife? You can't mean it. That mealy-mouthed little hypocrite, a vicar's wife? She'd say anything about me, she never forgave me for being made tennis captain instead of her.

Kit Tennis captain? Mrs Temple? Well, if it's any consolation, I shouldn't think she plays tennis any more — she's spread a bit since then. I rather gathered that you hadn't been bosom pals. That's probably why she remembers you so clearly. But then, the scandals of our youth do tend to stick in the mind.

Claire What scandal? Grandmother's death was a tragedy, not a scandal.

Kit Millicent remembers it as a rather convenient tragedy.

Claire That little scholarship girl! Millicent Clegg was a malevolent little bitch at fifteen, and evidently, she still is.

Kit Ah, a scholarship girl, was she? Well, that explains a lot. Your grandmother, on the other hand, owned the big house. I've no doubt your Grannie regarded the young man as "a bit of rough".

Claire What young man?

Kit Oh, come on, Claire, with a woman like you, there's always a man in it somewhere. Besides, what is the point of denying it? It was the talk of the fifth form, the only exciting thing to happen all term. Your grandmother was a school governor; without her influence you'd have been expelled. She managed to hush up the whole thing, didn't she? Getting rid of the young man would have been the easiest part, I imagine. One mention of the police and you wouldn't have seen him for dust. By the way, had you told him you were only fifteen, I wonder? Anyway, Grannie persuaded the headmistress to keep you on till the end of term, and then she would send

you to a Swiss finishing school. Who would have thought that poor old
Grannie would have a fatal accident? Just in the nick of time? Not only did
you escape Switzerland, but you did quite nicely out of Grandmother's
will. That is, according to Millicent and the fifth form.

Claire My God! You've got a nerve. You come into my house and repeat
a lot of vicious tittle-tattle from a crazy old woman and a venomous gossip
like Millicent. If you think you have the right to accuse me of two murders,
why don't you go to the police?

Kit Because we both know that none of this would stand up in court.

Claire Then what is your game, blackmail?

Kit I'm not trying to blackmail you.

Claire Then what do you want?

Kit I just want to make sure that there are no more accidents.

Claire What?

Kit I just want you to know that I'm watching you, remember that, and I see
no reason why David's ulcer shouldn't heal quite quickly.

Claire David? What has David to do with it?

Kit I'm concerned about his health and ——

Claire You're mad! What possible reason would I have for harming David?

Kit I don't know, a number of possibilities come to mind. Given your track
record, another man is the most likely explanation. On the other hand, he
may suspect that you have been writing those articles about the Research
Centre.

Claire I have been writing them?

Kit OK, supplying the information, then. You have contacts in the publishing
world. I bet it pays a lot better than cookery tips.

Claire Have you finished?

Kit Not by a long chalk. I know you, Claire, and I don't underestimate you.
You are clever and murder has become a game to you. An exciting game,
a way to pit your wits against the rest of us. Well don't try it, Claire. I'm
warning you. You won't get away with it, not this time — I shall see to that.

Claire Get out! Do you hear me? Get out of here and don't come back.

Kit I'm going. I shall be back, because I'm watching you, Claire, and don't
you forget it.

Kit exits

Claire is left fuming

CURTAIN

SCENE 2

The following day. Early afternoon

When the CURTAIN *rises, Claire is working on the computer. Some recently-printed sheets lie on the desk near her. A telephone is ringing insistently, somewhere in the house*

Beatie pokes her head around the door L

Beatie The phone's ringing, Claire.
Claire I can hear it.
Beatie I didn't like to answer it. Shall I?
Claire Feel free.
Beatie (*pleased*) Oh, right.
Claire And if it's for me, I'm out.
Beatie Out, right. I'll take a message.

Beatie bustles off, delighted to be of use

Claire gets back to work

David comes in from the garden

David Did I hear the phone?
Claire Yes, Beatie's getting it.
David It might be for me.
Claire (*with barely concealed impatience*) Why don't you go and see?
David Right, I will … No, on second thoughts, I'll leave it to her. She likes to feel useful. I expect she'll call if it's for me.
Claire (*answering automatically and trying to concentrate*) Yes, I expect she will.
David Busy writing, I see.
Claire Evidently.
David What is it this time, a recipe or a short story?
Claire Neither, it's an article.
David Really?
Claire About the press.
David You mean press as in newspapers?
Claire Your friend, the celebrated Christopher Kelly, gave me the idea. Arrogant bastard — he's too big for his boots if you ask me.
David Occupational hazard.
Claire Maybe, but I'd love to see him taken down a peg or two; nobody deserves it more. Mind you, they probably won't print it. They don't take kindly to criticism when it's directed at them.

David Never mind, worth giving it a go.

David drifts off to the garden

Claire gets going again

Beatie enters

Beatie It was the hospital.
Claire Oh?
Beatie About David's tests. They can fit him in tomorrow.
Claire So soon?
Beatie They've had a cancellation.
Claire I thought it would be next week at the earliest.
Beatie I knew you'd be pleased. The sooner he has the tests and we find out what's wrong with him, the better, eh?
Claire (*thoughtfully*) Yes.
Beatie Shall we call him in and tell him? (*Calling*) David …
Claire No. Leave him, he's busy in the garden; I'll tell him when he comes in.
Beatie Oh, very well, dear. Oh! My rock buns, they'll be ruined.

Beatie dashes off

Claire picks up the printed sheets, gets up from the desk and strolls round the room, making corrections on the sheets. She stops by the fireplace and sniffs. She looks around for the source of the smell, then lifts an ornamental bowl from the shelf and sniffs it. She looks at it with distaste

David enters from the garden

Claire David, what's in this bowl? It smells foul.
David Oh, sorry, dear, it's quite harmless.
Claire If you've finished with it give it to Beatie, she can give it a good wash.
David Good idea, she'll enjoy that.

Claire gives David the bowl, returns to the desk and starts typing. David sniffs the bowl and absentmindedly puts it down on a table

Who was that on the phone? Was it for me?
Claire I'll tell you later. (*She resumes her work but can't concentrate because David is hovering*) David, weren't you going down to the village? You said you needed something for the garden, twine or something.

David Oh, yes, twine, that was it, I knew there was something. I'll go now, shall I?

Claire doesn't answer

Yes, I'll go straight away. Anything you want? No?
Claire No. Thank you.

Beatie enters

Beatie I caught them, just in time.
David What?
Beatie My rock buns. Just on the turn, they were. But I like them a bit crisp.
David I'm just off to the village. Anything you want, Beatie?
Beatie No dear, thank you.
David Right, well, I'm off.
Beatie No, wait. It's such a lovely afternoon, I think I might come with you. Just for the walk.
Claire (*quickly*) I wouldn't do that, Beatie.
Beatie Why not?
Claire David walks so quickly, you'd never keep up.
Beatie Yes, but …
Claire Besides, it's so hot, you'd be exhausted. Why don't you take one of the garden chairs under the trees, sit in the shade and relax? You've been on the go all day.
Beatie Oh, well that does sound nice; perhaps I will.
David I'll see you later, then.
Claire You'll be back for tea?
David Rather, couldn't miss Beatie's rock buns.
Claire Four o'clock then.
Beatie There's no need to hurry, dear, we'll expect you when ——
Claire Beatie, you're the one who insists on regular meal times.
Beatie I know, but ——
Claire Four o'clock.
David I'll be back, see you later.

David exits

Claire (*lifting the soiled bowl and holding it out to Beatie*) David's been at it again.
Beatie Oh, no! He is naughty. You should put your foot down. It's so dangerous.
Claire He assures me it's harmless.

Beatie I'll give it a good wash out. (*She takes the bowl*)

Claire goes back to her work

Beatie looks round the room for a moment

Sorry to interrupt you again, dear, but you haven't seen my glasses?
Claire Beatie, why should I have had your glasses? (*She rests her head in her hand*)
Beatie I didn't say you'd had them, dear. (*She notices Claire's attitude*) Claire, are you all right?
Claire Why shouldn't I be?
Beatie You seem so strung up. I expect it's the heat, so oppressive. Shall I get you an aspirin?
Claire I don't need an aspirin, thank you, Beatie.
Beatie I shouldn't be surprised if we had a storm later, and we all know how you hate thunder. Still — this weather's bound to break soon.

Claire ignores Beatie

Perhaps it's your eyes — all that close work in front of the screen. You ought to get them tested.
Claire There is nothing wrong with my eyes.
Beatie We often don't notice, and when you get to a certain age ... I was only saying to Kit, just yesterday ——
Claire Ah, yes, Mr Kelly.
Beatie Charming man, isn't he, such a laugh? I was just thinking, he doesn't know anyone around here yet, except us. Wouldn't it be nice to have a dinner party, introduce him to some of your friends? Nothing elaborate — I could make one of my special ——
Claire (*her patience exhausted*) But we don't know that you're going to be here much longer, do we?
Beatie Oh, that's all right, I don't mind staying on and doing the cooking.
Claire Beatie, you seem to have forgotten this is my house. If I decide to give a dinner party, I shall decide what to serve, and who to invite.
Beatie Of course, dear. I didn't mean ——
Claire And it certainly won't be Mr Know-it-all Kit Kelly! You and David! What is this family obsession with the man? Who does he think he is? Coming here and lecturing us all as if we were ignorant peasants!
Beatie (*stung into a sharp reply*) Oh, well, personally I enjoy an intelligent, well-informed conversation, for once. You must remember, we don't all have your exciting, clever London friends.
Claire London friends? What are you talking about?

Beatie (*realizing she has said too much*) Nothing. I just meant that I know you have a lot of smart London friends, that's all.

Claire Oh no, you meant more than that, didn't you? Don't stop now, what exactly did you mean?

Beatie (*very upset*) Very well, but always remember, Claire — you started this, not me.

Claire Well?

Beatie All these trips to Mrs Thornton; very convenient, aren't they? Nights alone in London? Theatre trips? Getting your hair done? Why it's as plain as the nose on my face. You may pull the wool over David's eyes, but you don't fool me.

Claire So that's what you think of me? Well, I'm not surprised — I've known you resented me from the day David and I were married.

Beatie (*bursting into tears*) That's not true; I've tried, I've done my best …

Claire You had it all planned, didn't you, from the moment poor old Jim left?

Beatie No, please … !

Claire Oh yes, Beatie, face it, he left you, didn't he? He left you for another woman, and a bit of peace. All this "My poor Jim", and "Before I lost my poor Jim"… You lost him all right, but you've let everybody think you're a widow.

Beatie How can you be so cruel?

Claire When that poor devil left, you had it all planned, didn't you? You were going to move in on David, weren't you? But he spoilt your little scheme by marrying me, and you've been trying to get your feet under my table ever since.

Beatie Stop it! Stop it! I won't listen to any more of this.

Claire Oh, yes, you will. It's long overdue. Coming here, taking over my house, my husband, my marriage …

Beatie Marriage! What sort of a wife are you? You've driven one husband to suicide and now you're trying to poison my brother.

Claire Poison!

Beatie Yes, poison. Well it amounts to the same thing. I told you, he needs regular, simply cooked meals and a restful home. And what does he get? Hasty snacks at all hours and you constantly gadding about.

Claire Ho! So suddenly you're the expert. If you were such a model wife, how come Jim looked elsewhere?

Beatie (*trying to compose herself*) I — I don't know how this started; perhaps it's just as well it did. I never knew before just how much you hated me. You are right, of course, Jim did desert me. A woman like you, Claire, can't know what that's like for an ordinary woman like me. He was all I had, you see. I've never wanted to face the hurt, and pretending he was dead was a way of not having to think about the pain. It was a harmless little deception, but you can't even allow me that.

Claire Well then, there's nothing more to be said.
Beatie No. (*She goes to the door*) Would you ring for a taxi for me, please? It will take me about ten minutes to pack.
Claire For God's sake, Beatie, don't be so melodramatic. I'll run you to the station. Or if you can't bear me, David will.
Beatie Thank you. I prefer a taxi.

Beatie exits

Claire follows Beatie to the door. She comes back and picks up the dirty bowl and we see a smile of quiet satisfaction cross her face

CURTAIN

SCENE 3

Half an hour later

When the CURTAIN *rises, Beatie is sitting on the sofa. She is dressed for travelling, her handbag on her lap and her suitcase at her feet. She has been crying but is now composed. Claire is standing at the window. There is a charged silence between them. They are waiting for the taxi*

David enters through the door L

David Well, here I am, even a little bit early. By the way, darling, I met Kit in the village. He seemed at bit of a loose end, so I invited him back to sample Beatie's rock buns. He's coming straight up.
Claire (*drily*) Oh, how nice.
David I didn't get the twine, the garden centre … (*He notices Beatie's suitcase*) Hallo, what's this? You going somewhere, Beatie?

Beatie doesn't answer. David looks from one woman to the other and catches the atmosphere

Claire?
Claire Beatie's taxi will be here at any moment. You'll want to say goodbye. Excuse me will you?

Claire exits

David Taxi? What's she talking about? What do you need a taxi for? If you want to go anywhere you only have to ask, you know that, Beatie.

Beatie I prefer a taxi, if you don't mind. I like to be independent.
David Oh dear, have you and Claire had words?
Beatie You could call it that.
David What about?
Beatie You must ask Claire.
David Oh, come on, Beatie, it can't be as bad as all that. Surely you could kiss and make up?
Beatie I'm afraid not, David. I only wish it was that easy.
David But what's happened?
Beatie I don't know how it started, but we both said a lot of things better left unsaid, I daresay. A lot of things we didn't mean.
David Well, there you are then. Come on, take your coat off and let me call Claire.
Beatie No. Things are better left as they are for now. We both need time to get over it. If I stayed, I should only get on Claire's nerves. I fuss and fidget, I know I do. I can't help it. I don't mean to irritate — it's just my way.
David Oh Beatie, my dear — I do wish ...
Beatie Yes, dear, I know ... Don't say anything, or I shall start to cry again — mess up my face.

David hugs Beatie close. She smiles up at him and blows her nose

The doorbell rings

That's my taxi. Mustn't keep it waiting. Goodbye, David, my dear. It's been lovely. Thank Claire for having me, won't you. (*She goes towards the door and turns*) David, you will look after yourself, won't you?

Beatie and David exit, David carrying Beatie's suitcase

There is a pause

Claire enters with the tea tray — on which is a plate of rock buns as well as the tea things — and puts it on the table behind the sofa. She plumps up the cushions on the sofa where Beatie has been sitting and places a small table in front of the sofa. She lays out the tea cups on the small table

Kit appears at the window, mopping his brow with a handkerchief

Claire Oh, it's you, such a pleasure. David told me you were coming.
Kit Somewhat reluctantly, I assure you, but David insisted.
Claire If he hadn't invited you I should have done, in due course. This is a small village and I don't invite gossip. I've had enough to last me a lifetime.

Kit I'm glad to hear that.

Claire As for the conversation we had yesterday: that's all it was, really, gossip. Best forgotten, I think. A storm in a teacup. (*She holds up a cup*) Now do sit down. I expect you're feeling the heat; the rest of us are.

Kit I came round by the garden because there seemed to be a great deal of activity on your doorstep. Is Beatie leaving you?

Claire Yes, her taxi has just arrived.

Kit Rather sudden, isn't it? David didn't mention it.

Claire David didn't know.

Kit He didn't know?

Claire Beatie has a habit of making up her mind on the spur of the moment.

Kit Really? She doesn't strike me as the impulsive type.

Claire No? But then you don't really know her, do you? It's easy to misjudge people on short acquaintance, don't you agree? One so often underestimates them.

Kit is puzzled. He feels that Claire is up to something, but can't guess what

David enters carrying the sugar-bowl

David (*to Kit*) Oh, you're here, jolly good. Claire looking after you, I hope? I've just been seeing Beatie off — she wished to be remembered to you, by the way ... (*To Claire*) Darling, you forgot the sugar. (*He puts it on the tray*)

Claire Now then, how about some tea?

David Splendid; dying for a cup.

David's choice of words puts a sudden thought into Kit's head. He looks hard at Claire. She smiles pleasantly at him, and pours him a cup of tea

Claire Strange, isn't it, that tea should be so refreshing on a hot afternoon? (*She holds up the sugar spoon*) Milk? Sugar?

Kit Two, please.

David You being here has sparked off Claire's muse, you know.

Kit What?

David She's been pounding the word processor all afternoon. Blasting off against the press. An indignant blare on the trumpet, eh, darling?

Claire More of a discordant squeak. Kit's tea, David, would you mind.

Claire hands a cup to David who puts it on the table beside Kit

I hope that's how you like it. Milk, and two sugars.

Kit Thank you, that's fine.

Claire Pass the rock buns, darling, please.

David passes the plate to Kit, who helps himself and then puts the plate of buns on the table in front of the sofa. Claire, meanwhile, pours tea for herself and David

Kit Thanks. What particular aspect of the press are you attacking?
Claire Their arrogance.
Kit Arrogance — ah, well you're certainly on safe ground there.
Claire You agree, then; that's surprising. You see, I'm trying to make the point that it's the duty of the press to report things as they happen. Your tea, David.

David takes a cup from the tray and moves to sit on the sofa

(*Sharply*) David! You've got the wrong one. That's mine.
David Is there a difference?
Claire You know you like more milk than I do.
David Sorry, darling. (*He returns the cup to the tray and lifts the other which he takes to the table in front of the sofa*)

Kit gazes at the tea in disbelief, realizing what is happening

David sits, helps himself to a bun and begins to munch it

David But isn't that just what the press do, Claire, report the facts as they happen?
Claire Not always; in fact my argument is that far from just reporting the facts, they now direct events and then create a body of public opinion. A case of the tail wagging the dog.

Claire now brings her own cup to the table below the sofa and places it next to David's cup. She then returns to the tea table and fills the teapot from the hot water jug

During the following David lifts his cup and appears to be about to drink. Kit, watching him, is mesmerized

Public opinion is now whatever the press decides it should be. And the worst of it is, the public either doesn't notice, or doesn't care that it's being manipulated. Drink your tea, David, while it's hot — you too, Kit.
David There's something in what she says, don't you think, Kit?
Kit What?

Kit can't concentrate on anything except David's tea. David is again about to sip his tea but replaces the cup on the saucer in order to answer Kit

David About the tail wagging the dog. I mean, every story these days gets massive press coverage — so much so that it's bound to shape public opinion, and can't help but steer events.

David picks up Claire's cup which is beside his. He takes a long swallow

Claire David! You're drinking my tea.
David Am I, darling? Oh, sorry, here, you have mine.

David passes his own cup over the back of the sofa to Claire. Kit smiles with some satisfaction at Claire

Kit (*raising his own cup in a toast to Claire*) Drink up, Claire; as you say, "So refreshing on a hot afternoon." (*He watches her mockingly*)

David contentedly eats his bun and drinks his tea. Claire stares at Kit and then slowly raises the cup to her lips. Kit nods encouragingly. At the last minute Claire fumbles the cup and spills the tea

Kit Hah!
Claire Oh! How stupid of me.
David Dear, oh dear, butter fingers.
Claire Damn it, it's all down me, I'm soaked. So's the carpet.
David (*taking out his handkerchief*) Not to worry, no use crying over spilt tea. Let's mop you up. (*He moves to help Claire*)
Claire David, stop it, can't you see it needs more than a hankie.
David I'm doing my best, darling.
Claire (*pushing David away*) No, this is ridiculous, I'm soaked, I shall have to go and change. If you want to make yourself useful, look after Kit — give him some more tea or something.

Claire runs out

David Oh dear, women! She spills her tea and somehow it's all my fault. Take no notice, she's been like a cat on hot bricks all day; must be the heat.

Kit moves quickly to the door to make sure that Claire is out of earshot

The sky slowly darkens throughout the following as the promised storm approaches

Kit David, I must talk to you. We haven't much time.

David What's that? You don't have to rush away, do you?

Kit No, not that — Claire, she may come back at any minute. You have to listen to me.

David Of course. You're being very mysterious, I must say.

Kit That wasn't an accident. She spilt the tea deliberately.

David Really? What on earth for?

Kit She couldn't drink it. It was poisoned and she knew it.

David Poisoned! Claire's tea was poisoned?

Kit It wasn't her tea, it was yours; you switched cups.

David I did? Oh, yes, that's right. So I did.

Kit The poison was meant for you.

David What! What are you saying?

Kit Claire is trying to poison you.

David Oh, now, don't you start as well — I've had all I can take from Beatie.

Kit I'm serious, you must believe me. She's been poisoning you with small doses for some time; this afternoon the dose was meant to be fatal.

David Fatal! Fatal! Oh, I say, (*He starts to laugh and then sees the desperate look on Kit's face*) My God! You really are serious, aren't you? But my dear chap, why would Claire …

Kit Because she's done it before. Twice that I know of. She killed her grandmother and her first husband, and now she's tried to kill you.

David (*stunned*) But why?

Kit She gets a kick out of killing, don't you see that? And every time there's a legacy to go with it, just to add to the spice.

David But my dear chap, I haven't got a penny. Well, a few thousand in life insurance, I suppose — certainly not enough to kill for.

Kit It's enough. You don't have to take my word for it — there are other, well-documented cases, people who've killed for just a few pounds.

David But why now, why this afternoon?

Kit Because you were going to have tests; they'd have found out you were being poisoned. Don't you see? She couldn't afford to wait.

David No! There has to be some mistake …

Kit Why do you suppose she got rid of Beatie? You weren't expecting her to leave, were you?

David No, but … No, damn it. It's nonsense. If I'd died they would have found out I was being poisoned anyway. She couldn't have got away with it.

Kit She could, she could, and it would have been all my fault. (*He fishes his handkerchief from his pocket and starts mopping his brow*)

David Your fault?

Kit I gave her the idea, God forgive me.

David I don't understand.

Kit (*sitting on the sofa*) I gave her the idea for another accident. The first afternoon I was here — you remember, the dirty teacup? (*During the following he shows signs of finding it difficult to catch his breath*)

David The dirty cup? No sorry, it wouldn't work; everyone knows that Claire makes a point of washing everything very carefully. Nobody would believe she'd have an accident with a dirty cup.

Kit Not Claire, Beatie! It would have been blamed on Beatie's poor eyesight.

David Beatie! Yes, I see. You think Claire deliberately picked a quarrel with Beatie to get her out of the way? Couldn't risk her being here? I say, you don't look too bright — is it the heat? Is all this too much for you? What can I get you?

Kit I'm fine, it's you I'm worried about. I've got my pills … (*He searches in his pocket for the pills and finally finds them. He tries to open the packet*)

David Here, let me help. (*He takes the pills from Kit*)

Kit I'm supposed to take two.

David pops two pills out of their foil wrapping into Kit's hand. He then goes and fetches Kit's unfinished cup of tea and hands it to him

David Here's your tea, wash them down with this.

Kit takes the pills and drinks the rest of the tea

Kit I'll be fine in a minute.

David God, what a mess! I can't take it in — I still can't believe that Claire would …

Kit (*with an effort*) You must believe it. You must go to the police, give them that handkerchief, get it analysed.

David The police. Oh, my God! Yes, you're right, but I can't ——

Kit There's something else you should know: those articles, about the Research Centre — Claire wrote them.

David Claire did? Are you sure?

Kit As sure as I can be. I've made a few phone calls; everything points to her. (*He closes his eyes*)

David Are you all right? How long do those pills take to work?

Kit Not long, as a rule, but I feel different, as if … (*He opens his eyes and sits up, suddenly realizing what has happened*) Oh, no … Oh, God! … I didn't realize … What a fool …

David It's not your fault old chap, just sit there quietly and relax.

Kit (*pushing himself to the edge of the seat*) You don't understand, I got it all wrong. It wasn't you, it was me! She's poisoned me! Help me, call a doctor, hurry!

David A doctor, yes. (*He goes to the door then slowly turns*) A doctor? No, I'm sorry old chap, he'd never get here in time.

Kit Quickly! He must!

David No. I assure you he wouldn't. I'm truly sorry, Kit. (*He regards Kit with cold interest*)

Kit (*focussing on David with difficulty*) It's not her at all, is it? It's you.

David 'fraid so. *Et tu Brute*, and all that. As I say, I'm truly sorry, but it had to be done. You were becoming more than just a nuisance.

Kit But you'll never …

David There won't be any suspicious circumstances. Just a simple heart attack. With your history, only to be expected. Nothing traceable, you see. You should have remembered — I'm the chemist, not Claire.

Kit Why?

David You had the infernal cheek to stick your nose into our affairs. You got it all wrong of course, but you were determined to stir up the mud. I couldn't let you do that.

Kit Wrong?

David Oh, yes, completely wrong. Claire wouldn't harm a hair of my head. You see, we go back a long time, Claire and I. That's right — I was the "bit of rough" her grandmother got rid of. She paid me off, to be exact — well, it amounted to the same thing. She gave me a choice. Enough cash to do my post-grad. in California — or prison. Naturally I took the money. Of course, before I left, I arranged Grannie's little accident. I was in California for years. Claire and I lost touch — past history — until I read about Nigel Thornton's business difficulties in an English newspaper, and there was a photo of him and his wife. I caught the next flight home. When the trial started to go pear-shaped, I was able to help.

Kit is now slumped on the sofa, but still breathing

Can you still hear me? I hope so.

Kit opens his eyes very slowly and tries to focus

Good, because there's something else you got wrong. Claire didn't write those articles: I did. Why? Well, you got that right, as it happens — it created a most effective diversion from the real leak. Now that the Russians have turned into great big cuddly bears, people assume there's no market for information. Quite wrong: there's a certain — network — I'm sure you know the one I mean — which pays better than Moscow ever did.

Kit makes a tremendous effort and manages to get to his feet. He takes a step forward and collapses to his knees, finally, sprawling at David's feet

There is a roll of thunder

David feels Kit's wrist for a pulse

Rain starts to fall heavily

David goes to the window and closes it

  Claire enters hurriedly. She has changed her dress

Claire David, the window, it's raining like —— (*She sees Kit's body*) Oh! What? Is he ...?
David I'm afraid he's dead.
Claire Dead. But ... Are you sure?
David A heart attack — I think.
Claire Oh, how awful ... So sudden.
David Poor chap ... Nothing anyone could have done, of course — his condition was obviously worse than we thought.
Claire Yes — of course. Should we send for the doctor — or the ambulance ...?

Forked lightning lights up the sky

David An ambulance — would be better. (*He turns to the door*)

There is a massive clap of thunder overhead. Claire screams. David puts his arms around her and holds her close. She shivers convulsively

  It's all right, my darling, it's all right. Nothing for you to worry about. I'm here, you're quite safe.

CURTAIN

FURNITURE AND PROPERTY LIST

ACT I
SCENE 1

On stage: Sofa with cushions
Armchairs
Occasional tables; one behind sofa
Desk. *On it*: computer, printer, pot of pens and paintbrushes, large brown envelope
Desk chair
Waste-paper bin
Pot plants
Ornaments including bowl

Off stage: Green foliage plant in a pot, corked bottle containing white liquid (**David**)
Tray of tea things, scones, etc. (**Beatie**)
Glass of white medicine (**Beatie**)
Clean cups, sugar-bowl (**Beatie**)

SCENE 2

Set: *On table behind sofa*: tray of drinks, including brandy and Scotch, and glasses

Strike: Green foliage plant, corked bottle
Tray of tea things, scones, etc.
Medicine glass

Off stage: Glass of medicine (**Claire**)

Furniture and Property List

ACT II
Scene 1

On stage: as ACT I, Scene 1

Off stage: Straggly bunch of garden flowers

Scene 2

Set: *On desk*: Printed sheets of computer paper

Scene 3

Strike: Bowl

Set: Handbag and suitcase for **Beatie**

Off stage: Tray with tea things and rock buns (**Claire**)
Sugar-bowl (**David**)

Personal: **David**: handkerchief
Kit: handkerchief, packet of pills

LIGHTING PLOT

Practical fittings required: nil
One interior plus exterior window backing

ACT I, Scene 1

To open: General interior lighting with morning light on exterior backing

No cues

ACT I, Scene 2

To open: General interior lighting with evening light on exterior backing

No cues

ACT II, Scene 1

To open: General interior lighting with early afternoon light on exterior backing

No cues

ACT II, Scene 2

To open: General interior lighting with early afternoon light on exterior backing

No cues

ACT II, Scene 3

To open: General interior lighting with early afternoon light on exterior backing

Cue 1	**Kit** moves quickly to the door *Slowly fade lights on exterior backing*	(Page 39)
Cue 2	**Claire**: "— or the ambulance…?" *Forked lightning on exterior backing*	(Page 43)

EFFECTS PLOT

ACT I